Poetic Vehemence

Eulabell Williams

BookLeaf Publishing

Presentation by *BookLeaf Publishing*

Web: www.bookleafpub.com

E-mail: info@bookleafpub.com

ISBN : 9789357699280

First edition 2022

DEDICATION

I dedicate this book to my dad and my son. To my dad who passed away I told you I would do great things. thank you for always believing in me even in times I couldn't believe in myself. thank for showing me how to stay strong and show no weakness when it comes to life. you did a great job raising me . To my son who has so much growing to do all I do is for you. I hope one day you look back on this book and understand the meaning. I love you and the future is in our hands.

ACKNOWLEDGEMENT

I would like to acknowledge book leaf publishing for this amazing opportunity to express myself and allow the world to express themselves along with me. thank you to everyone with any involvement in the international poetry challenge as well. thank you to my Mother, my sister, my brother ,my best friend, and my son & family that keeps me going.I really hope this book inspires people to believe in themselves.

PREFACE

This Idea of a poetry book came from a International writing 21 day challenge I saw online. they mentioned how you had to write a poem each day for 21 days and I thought about what a great idea that would be being that it was a strong point for me. The themes of these poems is feeling and basically allowing yourself to free feel through words. Each poem is originally written by myself. the purpose of this book is to help people understand that everyone has feeling and emotions because its human there is no need to hide how you feel for nothing or nobody, allow yourself to feel what life brings you.

LOVE VS THOUGHT

Look up to two things
My Heart and my Mind
But, the seem to crash
Before they collide
My heart tells me one thing
But, my mind just rejects
because when my brain speaks
The heart doesn't accept
They are working together
But enemies on teams
Who will I listen to?
My Heart or my Brain

Cant Change It

Nothing like a story
Thats never been told
Cover up the tears
With a smile of gold
But nothing hides the pain
When you begin to unfold
From all the pain and tears
You held in before
No-one knows me in reality
But yet they know what I did
YEAH! its different hearing of it
And going through it with me
All of the hurt will never be gone
I was born by myself and ima die alone.

Mind Blown

People tell you anything
To make you believe
Then when it falls through
The Blames on me
For have scene
What I should have foreseen
In-between time
Thin lines
That hides
In the nature of pathography
Like its graphing me
and tracing my brain
Little insane
From grave to dust
The lust
The love can over power the rest

INVISIBLE

The anger excites me
As I go through things that try to indite me
But I slightly
Believe its just my emotions that fights me
Yet I refuse to believe
What I see
So I confuse lies with reality
So intelligently dumb
And blind to the fact
That only 3 letters got my back
But then the evil attacks
Start sending the brain insane
As I try to think
Why is this happening to me
I replied
You let it build up inside
From letting the dream take advantage
Of life lies
So I cry
I go In rage
Throwing things
Sceaming...like that's helping my pain
But no-one will realize until that day
My body laying frozen
Then tears will fall like rain
Or will they.......

It Hurts

Shears like a bullet
Shreads like a knife
Either ends in death
Or you can keep your life
Everyone has to die
So what your living in vain
Or are you living a lie
so forcibly played
As if the sun turned 10 shades of grey
But whose to blame
like putting fire to the flames
But it'll remain
Nothing can change
Or will ir?

Falling

My faith has greatly exceeded its limit
Limitations so far gone
With the wind
Following the clouds so anxiously
As if the sky were waiting for it to react to it
The fact of how
Precious seeds sprout only to blossom into something beautifully great
Tribulating the thoughts of a mastermind in the act of imagination
Screaming for activity and opportunity no-one can give
spontaneous as a color but diligent as a black and white portrait
Betrayed as something unnatural but normal
Cautiously dragging immunity to the pores of waterfalls
Falling with such indictment that the world wouldn't recognize it
As if it were just one thing to live for rapidly towering the mind
Penetrating the thoughts of humanity and human nature
It's all purposely made to fall that way.

NO-UTURN

My heart is taking illegal turns
Trying to beat the green light as it should
But follow the yellow light and slow things down
Using the negative red light which means STOP
To constantly u-turn on that route
That has a sign that say NO U-TURN
Merging towards a trail of deceitfulness
That abandoned me at one time
While the happy trail was saying come my way
I constantly turned the wheel to stir
Twords that happy direction
But there's a exit on each end
Thats leads to destruction or construction of another life
I try to keep straight as the activities on the side
Are distracting and causes me to look another way
Forcing my brain to say lets go
But my heart say you can't
Because you know that's the way
That caused me to break
But my mind won't let go
WHY? because I been down that road
So many times before
It feels its the only way to go

Only way I know
So the continue to battle for which road
I will take
But only distance can tell

Why I write

I write
To fight
All things in minds sight
Things that overwhelm my brain
Driving it nearly insane
Just the intensity of life
While you ask why I write
To free concerns, worries, memories, issues
That caused tears to lay on the tissue
Put out for me
Through misery or joy
As I pour my so into a bottle capped tight
With all the implements that crate life
To shine through
For who shall we run to if this bottle overflows
With growth
To flood or run out
or maybe both
Now do you understand why I wrote?

Endlessly Ending

I hate when I get to a point where im like where to go what to do
Mind overwhelming thoughts are disgusting hateful things that rude
Mad at nothing but mad at something all im asking is what or who
Why does this happen to me and not you, you, or you
My mind works like a clock it ticks for hours and hours
I try to stop it before time runs out but I don't seem to have the power
I fill myself with things overdrawn my responsibilities
Then get mad when I start feeling the way im feeling
Happy! or that's just a metaphor nowadays
Its not a word in this world for all we know is hate
Im so angry, so, so angry I could fight a army
When really I just want to break down and cry and wish no-one knew me
But then I begin to think
I DONT EVEN KNOW ME....

Hiding

You hide under the disguise
This mask you wear
A glare of the real sight
Of the real you appear
Thought this was something new
But it never changed I just couldn't see
That this was always you
After all I did and do
You would think I would see the truth
But all you do is lie
And its obviously exposing
Unfolding all the pain I'm feeling
Thinking it's the truth
But in all reality
You hide under your disguise
The mask you wear
A glare of the real sight
Of you will appear

We've Fallen

I say so much
But obviously
It means so little
So why keep trying
If I only get the finger in the middle
Why care?
If you don't
Why love?
If you won't
I never dreamed
Of a day I would leave
But if I leave
Will I feel relieved
or damanged
Fixed
Or broken
Only time will tell
If we have time its getting real
I can't put up with to much
This on top of that when will it stop
Your supposed to be my happiness
Where my smile can sprout
You showed me I mean nothing
Thanks a lot

Being A Woman

Lipstick , pink flowers & Blush
Poodles , roses, a sweet gentle touch
Jealousy, mood swings, periods, kids
Nail shop, shopping malls, credit card , wigs
emotional , sweet , love, smiles
Cant live with them
Cant live without them

Am I so blinded by

Am I so blinded by love
That I really can't see
What this is really doing to me
Is it bringing me up
Or down to my feet
Im down for you but are you down for me
Am I the only one
Thats playing my role
Am I the only one who cares
Thats giving my all
Is this a one person relationship
Or is it for two
Or is it me and you
And a third person to
Are you just with me
Because you don't want me to hurt
Don't say yes please
That would just hurt worst
But that can't be the case
Its been proven so many times
Like when I thought you wanted to break up
But every time we got close
It wasted my time
Because you never let it get
That far down the line
Maybe its just me being insecure

because your fine as hell
And I know how females do
But what if your foot was in my shoe
Would you think like me to?

LOVEEE

I hear what you see
I taste what you smell
I touch what you hear
I smell what you
And I smell what you touch
Translation
I hear your thoughts
Taste your scent
Touch your heart
And smell your love
ILOVEYOU

A part of me

Apart of me leaves
Every time I have to find something new
loneliness drastically begging me
telling me , you need someone,
your mind fussing that you can't function
without a body next to you, around you
all the time, feeling unworthy not good enough
Wondering why things never work out
depressingly self shaming myself
because to me I am the problem
maybe im nt good enough
not pretty enough
not established enough
for someone to consistently love me
for someone to want to love me,
for someone to adore me
for someone to see me In their future
the law of nature is good things come to those
who wait but im constantly
asking why? why do I have to always wait
why can't no-one relate
to the way I feel
Love like I want to love?
Apart of me leaves
Every time I have to start something new

DONT DESERVE

My love isn't counterfeit
yet my heart gets thrown, tossed, & handled
Like a puck getting hit with a hockey stick
Why do I accept the pain
As If I deserve it
All I did was give my last
Thats what I shouldn't have done
I should've Kept what I had
Maybe I don't deserve to be treated right
Maybe ill always have to put up a fight
I won't ever be treated like a queen
Maybe I should just let people walk over my heart
Maybe I should go hide alone in the dark
Question is who would care?
When all think know is ill do that
And ill be there
Just feel like its me against the world.

A rare connection

How rare of it
Is it that someway
Im connected to you
I feel like I could just be a temporary fix
But a temporary fix
doesn't feel like this
your smile is different
the way you speak is different
the way you feel
it just all seems to good to be real

Liberty

Sometimes I feel as if I should give up
Power isn't as powerful when fulfilling the complications of life
Time reveals all but still somethings hide
in the shallow shadow of grief
Storytelling issues battling horror of devastation
in the time of need
Those who shall feed the greed of nature
Attacking solar definitions of hope and faith
only so many know and understand
but are these figures human?
Or is it a way of expression
Only those of one can understand
Do you understand?
do I understand?
Do any of us understand?
The free rights of our thoughts
that are so serious but unharmful
For the will of conquering such a life
is free , free, free
FREE AT LAST

Still

Droughting in sorrow but not in pain
but the pain incarcerates every part of my vein
That flows from my ring finger all the way to
my heart
Its not imagination but an imparable start
thoughts flowing like a river that's refusing to
stop
everlasting evil with sound that sounds of the
harp
BUT STILL
I second guess can it all be real
just the feel
or needy postures refusing to kill
BUT STILL
I constantly try to refill
And heal
everything that departs form or comes with the
deal
Yet they make it sound loud and cruel
when your body is still
But your soul is in the bloodiest pool
But who
Who are we to pull ourselves out?

Actions Speak Louder

Your words say so much
But what does your actions express
I may not be superwoman
But there is always an S on my chest
Its like giving your all
But you have to wonder what's left
NOTHING would be the answer to that
They say don't give up just be strong
But when everything falls apart
The days seem so long
I don't speak my mind
I write my thoughts in poems
My feelings confuse me
But I keep nothing less then a grin
Ill understand them one day
But until then.......

My Son, My King

I was at war with myself
so conflicted and restricted
I was so hurt so lost
living in negativity addicted
then I met you
who knew
you would revive me
someone to stick beside me
my heart and my masterpiece
Mommy have days when she can do better
when she want to give up
but the thought of you won't let her
you taught me more
then I could ever teach you
but being a mommy is natural
not something you plan to do
I want to do this forever
to watch you grow
watch you succeed
see who you grow to be
I cry, I laugh, I smile behind you
I worry I overthink
but Id lose my life behind you
to my handsome young man
mommy king
I want you to know you are all I need

I will be here for you forever and always
even after me and this temporary body part ways
my shining star my son
My # 1.

www.ingramcontent.com/pod-product-compliance
Lightning Source LLC
Chambersburg PA
CBHW051755130826
49812CB00033B/1155
9789357699280